THE SYRIAC MENOLOGIUM AND MARTYROLOGY

Translated by: D.P. Curtin

Dalcassian Publishing Company

PHILADELPHIA · PA

ISBN: 9781960069658 (Paperback)

Library of Congress Control Number:
Author: Curtin, D.P. (1985-)

Book design by J.J. Ripplestick

Printed by Ingram Content Group, 1 Ingram Blvd, La Vergne, Tennessee

First printing edition 2023.

The Syriac Menologium and Martyrology

Names of Our Honored Martyrs, the Victorious, with the dates when they assumed their crowns.

Month of Canoun (at-Tani)- This is the 26th according to the Greeks. The first martyr in Jerusalem, Stephen, the apostle and leader of the martyrs.

✠ Canoun 26 [December 26th]- John and James, apostles in Jerusalem

✠ Canoun 27 [December 27th]- In the city of Rome, Paul the apostle, and Simon Peter, chief of the Apostles of Our Lord.

✠ Canoun 30 [December 30th]- Hermes the exorcist, was martyred in the city of Bologna

Canoun (al-Awwal), second month [January]

✠ Canoun 6 [January 6th]- On the day of the Epiphany of Our Lord Jesus at Heliopolis, also Lucian

✠ Canoun 7 [January 7th]- At Melitene, Polyeucte, and on the same day, Heraclee, a village in Thrace, Qnodinos the martyr, and at Nicomedia, there was Lucian the priest.

✠ Canoun 8 [January 8th]- At Nicomedia, Philorama

✠ Canoun 13 [January 13th]- At Antioch, Zebinos

✠ Canoun 14 [January 14th]- At Nicomedia, Glycerius the deacon

✠ Canoun 19 [January 19th]- In the city of Nicaea, Coschonis, Zenon, and Meliouhpos, the first martyrs

✠ Canoun 20 [January 20th]- In the city of Nicomedia, Leontis, and on the same day in Nicomedia, Cyrica, Kindus, Bitius, Floros, and Felix.

✠ Canoun 22 [January 22th]- At Nicomedia, Polyeucte, Eupsychius, Clement, Primus, Lelos, and Dabsos.

✠ Canoun 24 [January 24th]- At Nicomedia, Babylas, bishop of Antioch and the three children martyrs

✠ Canoun 25 [January 25th]- At Nicomedia, Titus, Parilos, Saturos, and Mamaios.

✠ Canoun 26 [January 26th]- At Nicomedia, Bitos

✠ Canoun 27 [January 27th]- In the city of Nicaea, Polyacharpos

✠ Canoun 30 [January 30th]- In the city of Antioch, Hippolytus

Month of Sebat [February]

✠ Sebat 4 [February 4th]- At Antioch, Maximin, bishop of Antioch

✠ Sebat 7 [February 7th]- Candida

✠ Sebat 12 [February 12th]- In Alexandria, Candidos and the other martyrs.

✠ Sebat 16 [February 16th]- At Caesarea in Palestine, Panphi and Pamphilius the priest, and eleven other martyrs

✠ Sebat 23 [February 23rd]- In Asia, of the ancient martyrs, Polycarp the bishop, Aretos, Coschonis, Melanouhphos, and Zeno.

✠ Sebat 24 [February 24th]- At Nicomedia, Euhetis

✠ Sebat 26 [February 26th]- Callinica and Alexander, martyrs

Month of Adar [March]

✠ Adar 1 [March 1th]- At Nicomedia, Cyriacius and (He)sychios

✠ Adar 2 [March 2th]- At Caesarea of Cappadocia, Gordian the martyr

✠ Adar 4 [March 4th]- Amplumilos, bishop of Antioch, and on the same say in Nicomedia, Photos, Archelaus, Cirina and the other seventeen martyrs

✠ Adar 6 [March 6th]- At Nicomedia, Victorin

✠ Adar 7 [March 7th]- In Africa, a number of ancient martyrs, Perpetua and Saturnilos, and ten other martyrs

✠ Adar 10 [March 10th]- Cyril and Kinda

✠ Adar 11 [March 11th]- At Nicomedia, Gorgonius, and at Antioch, Agape, and in Jerusalem seven other martyrs

✠ Adar 12 [March 12th]- To Nicomedia, Madronis the priest, Zmaragdos, Migdonis, Hilaria, Eugenia, Maximos, Peter, Dorothea, and Romana

✠ Adar 13 [March 13th]- At Nicomedia, Modestus, the priest-martyr and twenty-one other martyrs. At Thessalonica, Fronton, martyred with three others.

✠ Adar 15 [March 15th]- At Alexandria, Kolontos the deacon

✠ Adar 19 [March 19th]- Bassus and Serapion

✠ Adar 25 [March 25th]- At Nicomedia, Doulas

✠ Adar 26 [March 26th]- At Heraclea in Thrace, one of the ancient martyrs, Macien

✠ Adar 27 [March 27th]- Philip, bishop of Antioch

Month of Nisan [April]

✠ Nisan 2 [April 2nd]- Solon the Greek, At Thessalonica, Chionia and Agapa, martyrs

✠ Nisan 3 [April 3rd]- In the town of Tomes, Chrestos and Pappos

✠ Nisan 4 [April 4th]- Theodule and Agathopus, martyrs

✠ Nisan 5 [April 5th]- In Alexandria, Claudianus and Didymas

✠ Nisan 6 [April 6th]- In the village of Sirmium, Irenaeus the bishop, and at Nicomedia, Cyriacius. This friday after Easter, where all the martyrs are remembered, in the town of Nisbis, Hermes the martyr, on the same friday as the passion.

✠ Nisan 7 [April 7th]- In Alexandria, Peleusis the priest

✠ Nisan 8 [April 8th]- In Antioch, Maxime and Timothy

✠ Nisan 9 [April 9th]- In Sirmium, Demetrius

✠ Nisan 10 [April 10th]- In Alexandria, Apollonius

✠ Nisan 11 [April 11th]- In Salona, Dominion the bishop

✠ Nisan 13 [April 13th]- In the city of Peramon, among the ancient martyrs, Cyril the bishop, Agathonica, and Paul

✠ Nisan 16 [April 16th]- In Corinth of Achaea, Leonidos, and eight other martyrs

✠ Nisan 18 [April 18th]- At Salona, Septimius and Hermogenia

✠ Nisan 19 [April 19th]- Rufus the martyr

✠ Nisan 20 [April 20th]- In Antioch, Prosdoqas, Bernice, and Domnius

✠ Nisan 21 [April 21st]- At Alexandria, Aristos the priest

✠ Nisan 24 [April 24th]- At Nicomedia, Anthimo the bishop, and five other martyrs

✠ Nisan 28 [April 28th]- At Nicomedia, Eusebius the priest, Karalampos the priest, and two hundred and sixty-eight other martyrs.

✠ Nisan 29 [April 29th]- At Alexandria, Germain the priest

✠ Nisan 30 [April 30th]- In Aphrodisias, in the country of Caria, Dodotos and Rodophanus

Month of Iyyar [May]

✠ Iyyar 2 [May 2th]- According to the Greeks in Alexandria, Saturninus

✠ Iyyar 3 [May 3th]- At Melentine, Helpidis and Hermogena, martyrs

✠ Iyyar 4 [May 4th]- At Nicomedia, Antoninius the martyr

✠ Iyyar 5 [May 5th]- At Alexandria, Tetimis and Heros, bishop of Antioch

✠ Iyyar 7 [May 7th]- At Nicomedia, Flavius and four other martyrs

✠ Iyyar 10 [May 10th]- At Nicomedia, Acace the martyr

✠ Iyyar 11 [May 11th]- At Constantinople, Maxime

✠ Iyyar 12 [May 12th]- At Axiopolis, Cyrilla and six other martyrs

✠ Iyyar 14 [May 14th]- Aphrodisius and Serapion, bishop of Antioch

✠ Iyyar 18 [May 18th]- In Bithynia, Hercules and Paul

✠ Iyyar 19 [May 19th]- At Constantinople, in Byzantinum, Hesychis and other martyrs. And in Alexandria, Serapion the martyr and two other martyrs

✠ Iyyar 20 [May 20th]- Timothy and Polyeucte, martyrs

✠ Iyyar 21 [May 21st]- In Antioch, Proterius the martyr

✠ Iyyar 23 [May 23rd]- At Lystra, Zoilos the martyr, and the same day in Nisbis, Polycarp

✠ Iyyar 25 [May 25th]- In the village of Bobidouna, Flavian the martyr

✠ Iyyar 26 [May 26th]- In Alexandria, Eucharius the priest, and seventeen other martyrs

✠ Iyyar 28 [May 28th]- At Caeseara in Cappadocia, Cyrilla the martyr

✠ Iyyar 29 [May 29th]- In Antioch, Hesychis

✠ Iyyar 30 [May 30th]- Memory of Eusebius, bishop of Palestine

Month of Harizan [June]

✠ Harizan 1 [June 1st]- The first of the month according to the Greeks, in Antioch, Octavius and Zosimus

✠ Harizan 4 [June 4th]- At Bobidounia, Philip

✠ Harizan 5 [June 5th]- In the village of Tomis, Marcian and three other martyrs

✠ Harizan 6 [June 6th]- In Alexandria, Arius the priest

✠ Harizan 7 [June 7th]- Tirinus and fifty-seven other martyrs

✠ Harizan 8 [June 8th]- In Antioch, the first martyrs, Sositratus, Esperis, and Glycerius

✠ Harizan 10 [June 10th]- In the village of Tomis, Marcianus and forty-seven others

✠ Harizan 11 [June 11th]- In Caesearea in Cappadocia, Dio the martyr

✠ Harizan 12 [June 12th]- Meneos, Papias, and Mitaos, and in Caesarea in Cappadocia, Dio the priest, and in Isauria, Zenobis

✠ Harizan 15 [June 15th]- In Alexandria, Hierax, Philip, and ten children martyred

✠ Harizan 19 [June 19th]- In Antioch, Theodotus and Estatis, martyrs

✠ Harizan 20 [June 20th]- At Sirmium, Secandus

✠ Harizan 22 [June 22nd]- At Angora, Platon

✠ Harizan 23 [June 23rd]- At Laodicea, Menios

✠ Harizan 24 [June 24th]- Antigonis the Chorbishop

✠ Harizan 26 [June 26th]- At Laodicea in Phrygia, of the heretical faction of the Messaliens, in the persecution of those who returned to orthodoxy, united with the church and gave testimony, namely Theophilus the bishop and Philip, as well as five more

✠ Harizan 30 [June 30th]- At the Synod of Phrygia, the first martyrs- Democrtius, Secandus, and Dionysius

Month of Tammuz [July]

✠ Tammuz 15 [July 15th]-according to the Greeks, memory of James, bishop of Nisibis

✠ Tammuz 19 [July 19th]- At Synnada, Macedonius, Lampidus, Antigone, Jovinus, Victorinus, and Tatianus.

✠ Tammuz 30 [July 30th]- In the village of Nisibis, Adelphos and Gauis the martyrs.

Month of Ab [August]

✠ Ab 1 [August 1st]- The first of the month according to the Greeks, the martyrs who were numerous in the city of Antioch. That is to say, at Kerateia, the sons of Samoni, written in the Book of Maccabees. On this same day, the memory of Xystus, bishop of Rome, and in Nicomedia, Philip and four others.

✠ Ab 11 [August 11th]- At Nicopolis, Paul

✠ Ab 13 [August 13th]- At Synnados in Phrygia, Antonin

✠ Ab 14 [August 14th]- At Antioch, Bar Laha

✠ Ab 15 [August 15th]- At Nicomedia, the ancient martyrs, Philip and Antiochus

✠ Ab 16 [August 16th]- At Alexandria, the bishop Orion

✠ Ab 18 [August 18th]- At Emessa, Philantis and three others

✠ Ab 20 [August 20th]- At Alexandria, Dioscoridis the priest

✠ Ab 21 [August 21st]- One number of the ancient martyrs, Zoticus, and all the test of them

✠ Ab 24 [August 24th]- Marinus

✠ Ab 25 [August 25th]- Paulinus

✠ Ab 26 [August 26th]- Hysichis

✠ Ab 27 [August 27th]- Saba the priest and Alexander

✠ Ab 28 [August 28th]- At Sirma, Basilis

✠ Ab 30 [August 30th]- At Angora, Gaianus the martyr, and six others

Month of Aylul [September]

✠ Aylul 1 [September 1st]- the first of the month according to the Greeks, Euprepius, martyred with two others

✠ Aylul 2 [September 2nd]- In the village of Edessa, Habib, martyred by fire, and in Nicomedia on the same day, the ancient martyrs, Aphitarcin, Coscona, Zenon, Melanippus, and the sons of Theodota.

✠ Aylul 3 [September 3rd]- At Alexandria, Aristion the bishop

✠ Aylul 4 [September 4th]- At Angora, Marcellus and eight others

✠ Aylul 5 [September 5th]- At Alexandria, Nophius the priest

✠ Aylul 7 [September 7th]- Paulinus and four others

✠ Aylul 8 [September 8th]- Faustus the priest, Ammonis, and five other martyrs

✠ Aylul 9 [September 9th]- Silvanus

✠ Aylul 11 [September 11th]- Nemesius the priest, and seventeen others

✠ Aylul 14 [September 14th]- Ores the bishop, and Serapion the priest

✠ Aylul 15 [September 15th]- In Galatia, Seleucus and five others

✠ Aylul 16 [September 16th]- In Angore, Euseba

✠ Aylul 17 [September 17th]- In Chalcedon, Seleucus the Egyptian

✠ Aylul 18 [September 18th]- In Nicomedia, Oceanus

✠ Aylul 19 [September 19th]- In Alexandria, Castor and eleven other martyrs

✠ Aylul 20 [September 20th]- At Synnada, among a number of the ancient martyrs, Dorymedon

✠ Aylul 23 [September 23rd]- At Angora, the child who were martyred from their mother's womb

✠ Aylul 28 [September 28th]- Asteris (Esther)

✠ Aylul 29 [September 29th]- At Perinthus, Eutyches the bishop, Gensis, Sabinus, Eutyches, all martyrs.

Month of Trisrin al-Awwal [October]

✠ Trisrin al-Awwal 2 [October 2nd]- The second of the month according to the Greek, in Nicomedia, Eleutherius

✠ Trisrin al-Awwal 3 [October 3rd]- In Antioch, Zacheaus

✠ Trisrin al-Awwal 4 [October 4th]- Theotechnos

✠ Trisrin al-Awwal 7 [October 7th]- In Nicomedia, Kasarus

✠ Trisrin al-Awwal 8 [October 8th]- At Antioch, Pelagius

✠ Trisrin al-Awwal 9 [October 9th]- At Laodicea, Heracleon, and the priest Diodore, martyrs

✠ Trisrin al-Awwal 13 [October 13th]- At Chalcedon, Hadrios the bishop

✠ Trisrin al-Awwal 16 [October 16th]- In Asia, Decas and the other martyrs

✠ Trisrin al-Awwal 17 [October 17th]- Ignatius, the bishop of Antioch, one of the first martyrs

✠ Trisrin al-Awwal 20 [October 20th]- At Nicomedia, Eutyches and the other martyrs

✠ Trisrin al-Awwal 21 [October 21st]- Dasius, Gauis, and Zoticus, martyrs

✠ Trisrin al-Awwal 22 [October 22nd]- At Hadrianpolis in Thrace, Philip the bishop and martyr, and Hermas of the same city

✠ Trisrin al-Awwal 23 [October 23rd]- Herod the priest and and Dorothea

✠ Trisrin al-Awwal 25 [October 25th]- At Hieropolis in Phrygia, one of the first martyrs Cyrica and Claudianus

✠ Trisran al-Awwal 26 [October 26th]- At Antioch, one of the first martyrs, Silvanus and Marcianus

✠ Trisran al-Awwal 27 [October 27th]- At Eumenia, city in Phrygia, Tarsus, Polycarpus, and Gauis, as well as eight others

✠ Trisran al-Awwal 30 [October 30th]- At Nicomedia, Caledonian the martyr

Month of Tisran al-Tani [November]

✠ Trisran al-Tani 3 [November 3rd]- The third of the month according to the Greeks, at Caesarea of Cappadocia, Germain, Theophilus, and Cyril

✠ Trisran al-Tani 8 [November 8th]- Eusebius

✠ Trisran al-Tani 13 [November 13th]- At Perinthus, Hedistos the priest

✠ Trisran al-Tani 14 [November 14th]- In the same city, Theodotos and Demetrius, priests and martyrs

✠ Trisran al-Tani 15 [November 15th]- At Antioch, Secundus and Orentis, one of the first martyrs. And on the same day, in the city of Edessa, Samona and Gouria, martyrs

✠ Trisran al-Tani 17 [November 17th]- At Nicomedia, Ammonius, Diophilus, and Matrona, martyrs

✠ Trisran al-Tani 18 [November 18th]- At Antioch, Romanus

✠ Trisran al-Tani 19 [November 19th]- Maxime the chorbishop, Lucian the priest, and Chartaras

✠ Trisran al-Tani 20 [November 20th]- One of the first martyrs, Basil

✠ Trisran al-Tani 21 [November 21st]- At Melitene, Plotin and forty-nine other martyrs

✠ Trisran al-Tani 24 [November 24th]- At Caeseara in Cappadocia, Beronicianus. And in the city of Alexandria, Peter, the bishop and martyr.

This is the end of the martyrs of the west

The names of our honored dead, martyrs in the east

Abba, the first martyr, Dali the second martyr. Boulha, Hazat, Aphrahat and Menophilus, the first martyrs. Milos the bishop, and Aborsam and Sinai, all martyrs.

The names of the bishop-martyrs, who were put to death in the east

The names of our honored bishop-martyrs among the Persians: Simeon, Barbasmin, and Sahdost, bishops of Seluecia-Ctesiphon, the city of the Arameans. John, the bishop of Hormoz-Ardasir, city of the House of Houzoie, John and Shapur, bishops of Carca of the House of Zalok, Gadihab and Sabina, bishops of Beth-Lapat in the House of Houzoie, Boulida, Baradba and John, bishops of Perat of Maisan, Paul the bishop of Cascar, Hourman the bishop of Halwan, Nerse the bishop of Saharqart, John and Abraham, bishops of Arbela.

The names of the priest-martyrs: Abdhaicla, Hanina, Badboui, Paul, Zizi, Paul, Naqib, Adna, Isaac, Hourmizd, Hablaha, Badema, two priests of Seleucia-Ctesiphon, city of the Arameans. Longin, priest of Meskena, Sila, Bar Habsaba, Tirai, Sila, Abdisou, priests of Mahouze of the Arameans, Biba, Mari, Simeon, Papa, Isaac, priests of Houlsar, Andrew, Abdzakia, Joseph, Abraham, Andrew, Abraham, Bar Habsaba, Naqib, Adna, Simeon, John, priests of of the land of the House of Houzoie, Marsan, Papa, Aitamir, Bar Habsaba of Hadiab, Abu, Abraham, Peter, Pambak, Sousi, Papa, Sasan, Baras of the House of Garmai, Jacob, Addai, Noucria, Satra, Abraham, Isaac, Saripha, Mari of Seleucia, Jacob the first martyr of Tella-Salila.

The names of the deacon-martyrs: Papa, deacon of Helmin, Yabsin, deacon of Riasdar, Varan, Madian, deacons of Meskena, Abdisou, Isaac, Mari, Mari, Isaac, Abdisou, Jacob, Abdisou, Dadac, Kosrou, Maria, Malki, John, Abda, Naqib, Adna, Mela, Abdisou, Amaria, Addai, Hablaha, Sasi.

Other Titles by D.P. Curtin:

First Book of Ethiopian Maccabees (2018)
The Syriac Menologium and Martyrology (2022)
Book on Religious Exercise and Quiet by *Isaiah the Solitary* (2022)
Vision of Theophilus by *Cyril of Alexandria* (2022)
On Fate (De Fato) by *Albertus Magnus* (2023)
Fragments of 'Chronicle' by *Hippolytus of Thebes* (2023)
Life of the Blessed Theotokos by *Epiphanius Monachus* (2023)
Syriac Life of John the Baptist by *Serapion the Presbyter* (2023)